STAGE
5
BOOK 2

SMUGGLERS

John Townsend

228248 EN
Smugglers

Townsend, J

ATOS BL: 2.8
Points: 0.5   MY

"I've got good news and a little bad news," Miss Evans began. "The good news is that new chairs will arrive soon. We can't really afford them but they'll be far better than the old wobbly ones. I can't wait to get rid of those horrid yellow chairs. The bad news is ... we need to get them down to the storeroom. Any offers of help?"

"I'll do it," Asad said. "It won't take long."
"Thanks, Asad. You're an angel," Miss Evans smiled.

4

"He's not the only angel round here," Maya giggled. "I'll help him."

"Good for you, Maya. Now we've got a couple of angels," Miss Evans grinned.

"More like double trouble," Anna added.

The storeroom was full of junk.
"It's so messy down here," Maya groaned.
"It's a total muddle."
They stacked the chairs in masses of jumble.
"This floor isn't level," Asad said.

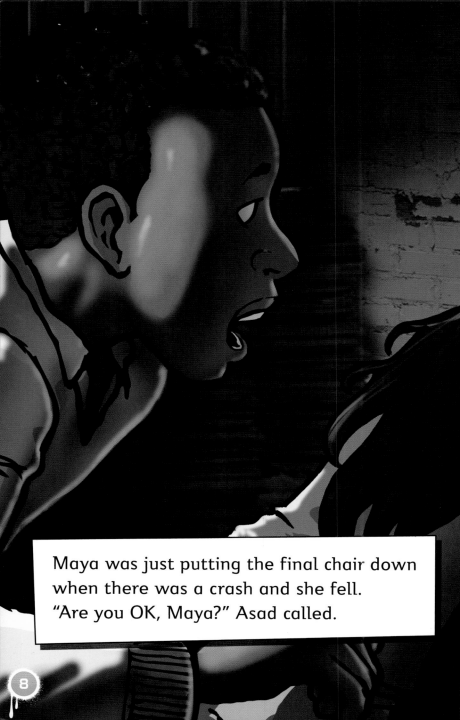

Maya was just putting the final chair down when there was a crash and she fell. "Are you OK, Maya?" Asad called.

"Yeah, but look down here," Maya cried as she stood up. "The chair leg went down a hole. A metal cover slipped off. It looks like there's a tunnel under it."

Asad got a torch and they peered into the tunnel.
"Shall we take a look down there?" he asked.
"Yeah, I'll wriggle down the narrow passage first," said Maya.

They began to crawl along the tunnel.
After a few twists and turns, it led to
a damp and smelly cellar.
"Hey, look over here," Asad called.
"There's an old wooden box and
a barrel."
Their feet crunched on gravel in
the darkness.

Asad slowly opened the box. Its dusty lid lifted with a creak. In the light from his torch, he saw a flash of gold.

"Wow, it looks like gold cups and lots of bottles," he cried. "Let's take some of this back and show Miss Evans. You bring a couple of bottles and I'll carry some cups."

Asad gave a yelp and said, "Don't do what I just did. I stepped in the middle of a puddle."

"My jeans can't get much wetter," Maya replied. "But it doesn't matter if we've found gold!"

After telling Miss Evans what they found, Maya and Asad showed Oz. He looked puzzled. "How did that stuff get hidden down there?" he said. "I'll make a few calls and get back to you."

Later

Oz ran into the room. "Maya and Asad are even better than a couple of angels," he cried. "Club OK is now on the news."

"That old tunnel led from the docks to a smugglers' den," he went on. "Long ago they used to smuggle stuff in the dead of night — and you found it. So it looks like we can now afford even more new chairs!"

CHECK

1. What did Miss Evans say was good news?

2. What was the bad news?

3. Who were happy to help?

4. What was it like in the storeroom?

5. Where did the tunnel lead?

6. What did they find in the old cellar?

7. Who once used the cellar as a den?

FIND

*Find the **verbs** to fill the gaps.*

1. They _____ the chairs.   (page 7)

2. There was a crash and she _____ .   (page 8)

3. A metal cover _____ off.   (page 9)

What's missing?

1. ill do it asad said it wont take long   (page 4)

2. are you ok maya asad called   (page 8)

3. shall we take a look down there he asked   (page 10)

*Find the **'le' nouns** to fill the gaps.*

1. "More like double _____," Anna added.   (page 5)

2. It's a total _____.   (page 7)

3. You bring a couple of _____s.   (page 14)

4. I stepped in the middle of a _____.   (page 17)

Which word in the story means

1. have the money to pay for?   (page 2)

2. two?   (page 5)

3. rubbish?   (page 7)

4. subway or passageway?   (page 12)

*Swap the word in **bold** for a new word that means the opposite.*

5. The storeroom was **full** of junk.

6. I'll wriggle down the **narrow** passage.

7. It led to a **damp** and smelly cellar.

8. My jeans can't get much **wetter**.